I'm a Girl ... That's Why!

by Reneé Rongen

a book in the

Fundamentally Female™
collection

edited by
Carol McAdoo Rehme

Kittleson Creek Press
10719 390th St. SE
Fertile, MN 56540

Fundamentally Female™ is a trademark of Reneé Rongen & Associates, LLC.
Edited by Carol McAdoo Rehme.
Cover Art by Annette Wood.
Graphic Design by Jeff Kale.

First Edition, November 2016
Second Edition, October 2017
Printed in Canada.

Visit www.reneerongen.com for links to contributors.

Library of Congress Control Number: 2016905749

ISBN: 9780988185616

To Elizabeth and Grace,

May you always be curious enough
to take risks and color outside the lines.

I am so proud to be your mom!

#Proud

#Upfront

Girls are different. It is that simple. And, as you grow into who you were created to be, like me you will find that women are different than men. We navigate the world differently, we think differently, and we act differently. That is okay. Actually that is great.

We have a need to question, a need to understand what's going on around us. Often, we internalize the actions or dialogues we observe. Between it all there are viewpoints, opportunities, advancements, and challenges to navigate.

Yet, through the years, I've had to defend and explain away my femininity to justify moving forward in sports, school, work, and even lifestyle. Along the way, I heard others echo my exact sentiments: "So, I'm a girl."

At some point, it seemed those words needed muscle, an exclamation point, or more confidence. I wanted my femininity to be a declarative sentence, a sentence of pride rather than an explanation of why I could not do or be something.

So, in this book you will hear my voice and the voices of amazingly talented young women authors and illustrators as they offer—without excuses—their stories, pictures, and words to declare, emphatically, *I'm a girl ... that's why!*

May you rise up to be strong women and strong examples. May you build each other up instead of tearing each other down. May you strive to push boundaries, seek answers, follow your hearts, and keep moving forward. May you honor your uniqueness and differences, the qualities that make you ... you.

And, when someone questions your premise (and they will), may you confidently look them in the eye and say, "Because I'm a girl, THAT'S WHY!"

RWR

5

#FindingOurselves

We live a different life from others;
sometimes we see ourselves as lower.

We are insecure about our looks
because they judge us like a book.

We are called names
and we are played like games.

Our hearts are hard to capture
just like a beautiful picture.

They'll never understand what we go
through until they step in our shoes.

But we are stronger than we seem;
we stick together like a team.

And we fight
for what we think is right.

Do not underestimate us women
just because you are men.

"Creativity is inventing, experimenting, growing, taking risks, breaking rules, making mistakes, and having fun."

~ Mary Lou Cook

#Imagination

My time disappears
to unknown places,
Chemistry and Government,
fleeing in unspoken phrases.

Long forgotten formulas
escaping my mind,
all that remains
are dreams to find.

My pencil scribbling,
filling pages with determination,
traditional to digital,
absorbed by my own creation.

Homework and classes
are no comparison
to the joy I find
in drawing out my mind.

#AllMine

Family is defined as blood-related individuals. My family is the people that I love and hold dear, the ones who have taken care of me with affection. My parents are not just my parents because they conceived me, but because they worry about me, nurture me, and want the best for me—not only for me, but also for their families and my siblings.

My mom is one who always keeps her head on straight. Who withstands frustrating and intense situations, situations that I would not know how to handle, while still maintaining the household.

My father is one who works with only three hours of sleep, every day, for twenty years. Despite the weariness and exhaustion, he perseveres for our sake all these years to support our family here and in the Philippines.

My aunt, who is more than an aunt, is one who experiences difficult events but always keeps a smile on her face.

Siblings are those I have a certain connection with, no matter the circumstance.

Despite the distance, my older sister is my sister and my older brother is my brother. The memories we made keep us together and make our relationship special.

With these individuals, I feel a sense of a loving home with its own side of bumps. These bumps are what defines us: unique and mine. My Pamilya is my family.

YOU CANNOT BLEND IN WHEN YOU WERE MEANT TO SHINE.

#PlayingTheCoda

They found a tumor. Mrs. Jeitz has pancreatic cancer.

I stare at the earth-shattering text, desperately wanting the words on my screen to be a Halloween-style prank. I am waiting for the "gotcha" I know will never come.

Norma Jeitz has been my piano/voice lesson teacher for some time now. But she is more than that. She is my mentor, my confidante, the reason I am where I am today as a musician and a person. A thin, feisty woman who knows exactly how hard to push and how much to say, she painstakingly pulled me out of my shell. She has given me confidence in my singing, my piano and flute playing, and in my day-to-day life as a woman. And now she has cancer.

I take my seat in pre-calc, knowing that I am about to fail this quiz. My mind is entirely elsewhere. Somehow I finish and get to my ear-training class. All the while, "what ifs" and "how comes" consume me. Later, I let my feet carry me back to my room. Somehow, piano books are in my hands, along with the key to the piano room. This is how I've dealt with every emotion for eleven years: I play them out.

It has been two weeks since I last played, and every wrong note feels like a direct insult to the years Mrs. Jeitz spent teaching me. Soon though, I come into my own. I reach for a new book, her gift at my high school graduation. Inside, inches from my fingers, is a note from Mrs. Jeitz. A lump forms in my throat as I reread her words. I scan the table of contents, knowing what I need to play: "Time to Say Goodbye," made famous by Andrea Bocelli.

During my freshman year our girls' choir, under the direction of Mrs. Jeitz, gradually perfected a gorgeous arrangement of this piece. The song meant something special to all of us. Ours was the last choir she directed; she retired at the end of that year. I begin the subtle melody, slowly, tentatively. As my fingers flit across the keyboard, memories and experiences with this favorite teacher flood my mind: my first voice lesson; her comforting words when I didn't make all-state choir; the pride in her eyes one year later when I did; entire lessons devoted to two or three measures of a single song; lessons devoted to conversations on any and every topic.

I learned as much from Mrs. Jeitz about life and choices as I did about music. To her, everyone was worth something, everyone had something to give. She found it and pulled it out of her students. Resistance was futile. She had been a constant presence through the most tumultuous years of my life. During one lesson, she just let me cry. For forty-five minutes I had sobbed at the piano, blubbering over the worst, most stressful day of my teenage life. She understood.

Now here I am again, three years later, crying at the piano. The song comes to a trembling end. The thought of Mrs. Jeitz getting sick and leaving everyone who loves her is heartbreaking. When I felt this hopeless in the past, piano was my escape. But it is also the main focus of my relationship with Mrs. Jeitz and playing will not separate me from this devastating news. Yet play I must; Mrs. Jeitz opened that door for me. Shutting the door on this, on her, on myself, is exactly what I can't do.

I shove the music books aside and begin to play what I feel. I create a moment within my whirlwind of desperation, a moment of acceptance. I can't control this disease; I can't control how long she gets to stay. But I can control this moment of creation. I cling to that.

#DarkThoughts

When night blankets the sky, I lie in bed and overthink everything. Thoughts bounce inside my head like a pinball machine:

● I lose way too many battles with myself. But I always win the war. I say, "I'm fine" more times than I can count, whether it's the truth or not. ● Sometimes I'm too emotional, and I beat myself up for it. ● I feel loved when people sincerely worry about me, when they reach out to me. ● I yearn for compliments, yet blush with embarrassment when I receive them. ● My spirit resides in my phone, as I glimpse into my life and others' from a different viewpoint. ● No matter how many times I tell myself I deserve someone better, my heart still yearns for the person I know is not good for me. ● I'm in love with the idea of love. ● My cheeks have been overwhelmed with grins, yet have felt the presence of thick tears. ● I'm delighted when I see people genuinely laugh, exploding into loud guffaws. ● My brightest smile pops out when I haven't seen the mirror in days.

And I know that all this is what makes me a girl.

THE QUESTION ISN'T WHO IS GOING TO LET ME, IT'S WHO IS GOING TO STOP **ME.**

~ AYN RAND

15

THERE ARE SOME PEOPLE IN LIFE
WHO MAKE YOU LAUGH A LITTLE
LOUDER, SMILE A LITTLE BIGGER,
AND LIVE A LITTLE BIT BETTER.

#Chaos

I want to forget. Yet how am I supposed to when
I don't even remember in the first place? Reset my
mind. Rewind the tapes of time to remember and
forget again. Become engrossed in the moment
that has every, and no, meaning. All. At. Once.

Calm my racing thoughts to keep up with my
gasping breath. Pull together to portray nothing
of my vague remembrance and forgetfulness.
Erase my thoughts. Take away the pain.

But it takes a hurting to heal and I put
the pain all on myself. I choose sorrow.
All this and I want to make it stop.

Stop! Make it STOP!

The pain is too heavy a burden. It makes me
weep to even ponder you and your twinkling.
Too far away, you're too far from my reach.

Why do I even try? What's its worth?

#12YearOldMe

I am not like other girls. I'm twelve. I'm 160 pounds. I'm 5'7". To top it all (get the pun?) my mom takes me to get my hair "trimmed," but ~~behind my back~~ without asking my opinion, she tells the hairdresser to cut my long shag into a pixie. Can you imagine? A pixie style makes me look like Mr. Potato Head with a toupee. Then, imagine me in leotards. Because that's what happens next. Me, in lycra (which shows EVERYthing) cut high at the thigh, desperately trying to suck in my stomach.

On second thought, it's too painful to imagine.

In tears, I approach the basement studio of Mrs. Maves for my first day of dance class. Short and stout beneath her tent dress, she invites me to join eight others—with their perfect sizes and lusciously long hair—who are already busy tumbling. Spry cartwheels, crisp roundoffs, agile hand springs …. Supersized girls like me don't learn this for fun in the backyard; they build forts with boys and dig for treasures in the woods.

"This will be fun, girls." Mrs. Maves' firetruck-red lips curve into a smile.

Yeah, right, I think. Fun for who?

She starts us on floor exercises—forward summersaults, backward summersaults—then lines us beside the long, mirrored wall.

Puh-leeze. Now I have to watch myself do this?

Sweat pours from my armpits as she teaches us ballet positions. The other girls laugh. I'm sure they're laughing ~~at~~ with me.

"Now, girls, we'll learn a 1920s dance. The Charleston!" Mrs. Maves squints through her fake lashes, assessing each member of her class.

As we start learning the steps—which (oh, goody!) we'll practice, perfect, and perform onstage for beaming parents behind flashing cameras—Mrs. Maves slips beside me, bobs her silvered head, and whispers in my ear.

"You are really going to be good at this!"

Stunned at her confidence in me, I listen intently. I grit my teeth and watch her every move. The Charleston, it turns out, is a sassy dance, from an era when women chewed gum and smoked cigars. A dance full of attitude.

Attitude. Now, THAT I have!

It's clear: The Charleston is ~~our~~ my dance. I concentrate on learning the steps. I will master this.

The half-packed auditorium didn't even faze me. The night of the recital, I was a 1920s flapper. With a beaded headband across the bangs of my sassy, pixie-perfect hair, I twirled the long strand of pearls around my neck and shimmied my full 160 pounds to each bouncing step. Despite the earlier humiliation of tumbling and ballet routines, I stood front and center—full of attitude—and led the other girls through the Charleston.

Believe me, I was fully aware of all the beaming parents clapping to the catchy beat of the music, laughing, cheering us on. And when I took my bow, singly, as the solo dancer, I glanced over at Mrs. Maves, who stood beside the stage curtain. Her brilliant blue-shadowed eyes crinkled as she gave me a slow, proud wink.

RWR

Do what you want & say what you feel.
Those who mind, don't matter and
those who matter, don't mind.
Dr. Seuss

I am the only teenager I know with a TBI. Sometimes I wish it never happened, but it did. I can doom myself forever or face the facts and say that my brain injury is just another special part of me. If the accident hadn't occurred, I would have missed out on special opportunities. I never would have met the many therapists who helped me get back up to speed at Children's Hospital in Denver. I never would have become a certified accomplished rider at Hearts and Horses Therapeutic Riding Center. I never would have been able to have my wish granted to visit all the Smithsonian Museums in Washington, D.C., with my entire family.

I never would have had to learn to work harder at absolutely everything I do. My life would have been very different and I would have been very different ... but it is all okay. I know I'm not exactly like anybody else, and I have learned to embrace that fact.

We should all embrace our differences. At times, we might wish to blend in, like I wish when my arm and leg braces get noticed. When I think negatively, I try to remind myself that my differences don't put me at a disadvantage; they make me special.

You are unique. I am unique. And, isn't it wonderful?

#Creation

God's greatest gift,

A sign for our existence,

The earth, so full of life;

Ten billion miles trodden over.

Numerous lives spun and unraveled each moment,

Never-touching circles, in a sea of faces we fail to recognize:

Prosopagnosia, a disorder of each victim

The world possesses.

Whispers pierce like blades,

Single words running through our veins,

Verbal surgery to capture thoughts

Now in the hands of demons who feed on innocent souls.

Corrupt, careless, ignorant ones,

Could we have ever overestimated you more?

Living not of this world but merely in it,

Shadows lurk not far behind, waiting to crumble the earth to dust.

Live
EVERY MOMENT

Laugh
EVERY DAY

Love
BEYOND WORDS

I' VE PROBABLY OWNED ABOUT **6000** BOBBY PINS IN MY **LIFE** AND DO **YOU** KNOW HOW MANY I HAVE **NOW?**

MAYBE 5.

#BeingFirst

He wants to say it. I know he wants to. I can tell by the sudden change of pace in his breathing, the quick inhale, pause, and slow exhale. Since it isn't his nature to take leaps of that nature, (I think he is more afraid than I am) I begin to play with the idea of speaking the words we both know were there. Those three tiny words. As I try to form them, I begin to understand the hesitation I see in his face, the hesitation that fills the pauses.

My breath catches, the calm before the storm. Why is this so hard? We both know exactly what needs to be said, but we're terrified. This is new to us. Suddenly, the light in his eyes flickers. He seems resigned, almost defeated. *He's waiting for me, I realize. This is my leap to take, not his. He knows how he feels and he is all too aware that I know. He is waiting for me.*

Even so, he speaks first, his syllables light and sure. I hardly hear him. As soon as his lips stop moving, words tumble from my mouth. "I love you." His eyes sparkle and he flashes his shy-boy smile. "I love you, too."

Later, when I dissect the evening, I realize what the flash in his eyes had been. Relief! He genuinely wasn't sure if his feelings would be reciprocated. Thinking of him, though, and all that he is, how can I not love him? It was right to say the words.

27

We all grow into the beautiful person that we're supposed to be.

Some earlier.
Some later.

~ Sandra Bullock

NEVER MISS A **CHANCE** TO MAKE A **MEMORY.**

~ Reneé Rongen

#FoodForThought

Beautiful Girl, you bit off more than you can chew.
I know it's hard to conceal what you have inside
of you. Don't you know it's unsafe to let your body
down? It has no escape.

Beautiful Girl, you were born to strive. The food
you eat will keep you alive. Don't shut yourself
down. Keep pushing and yearning until your health
is found.

Beautiful Girl, keep your head up high. Don't let
what you put in your stomach be discouraging in
your mind. It hurts to see you cry. Master your
trials and pains and I promise you'll survive.

Beautiful Girl, please put this thing to rest. You're
strong and independent and I know you'll pass this
test. Beat the disease. Release all your troubles.
Put yourself at ease.

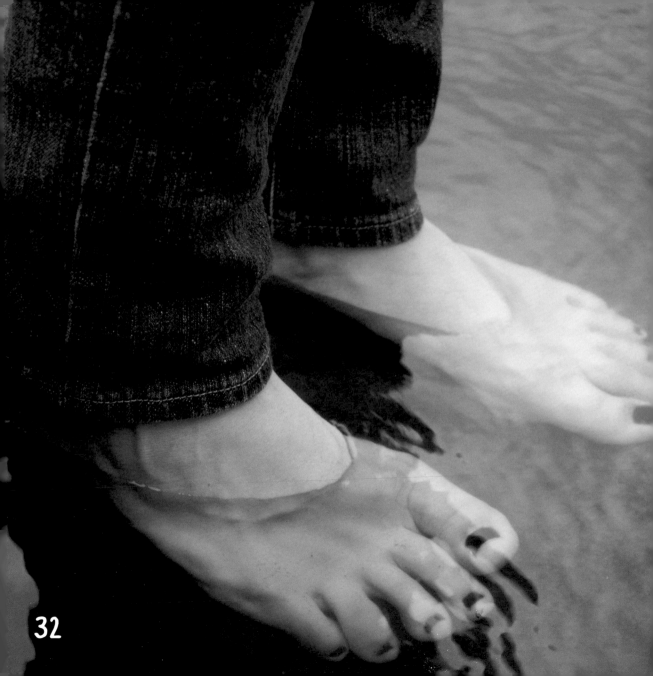

#CryMeARiver

I believe that it's okay to cry. Life is hard. Life is stressful. Sometimes it feels like life is against us. When we feel like we just can't do it anymore, like we just need to let it out, we cry. Sometimes there is enough for a river, sometimes a tear or two escapes.

Others might tell us, "Big girls don't cry." But that isn't true. Big girls, mothers, grandmothers, we all cry sometimes. And it's okay. Like rain cleanses the earth, tears clean our souls. Those tiny drops carry with them pain, sorrow, heartbreak, frustration, anger, loneliness, and the feeling that we are not good enough. They carry it all away, leaving space for happiness and confidence and the feeling that we are whole once again.

A good cry lets us know that life is good and gives us the strength to face a new day. So go ahead and cry. Let it all out. It's okay.

#BrainDamage

I'm homesick for the places I've never been.
I have a broken heart from someone who
doesn't even know I exist.
I'm lost,
I'm distraught,
I'm sick in the head.
I'm quickly dwindling my life away
by longing, waiting,
Suffocating.
I pine and yearn and love and desire
'til I eventually set my dreams on fire.

34

Your worth does not depend upon what others think of you.

35

#13YearOldMe

Drum rolllllllllll: I am officially a teenager!

What? Shouldn't there be more excitement? Don't I get more privileges? Shouldn't there be fewer rules? After all, I mean … I am thirteen! A teenager at last!

My girlfriends are coming over and we're going to levitate one of them using only our fingers.

"You're light. Light as a feather," we'll chant.

And, shhhh, one of my friends is bringing her Ouiji Board. We only sneak it in on monumental occasions and it doesn't get much bigger than official teendom! I'm counting on Ouiji to tell my future. I mean, my whole entire life is out there, just waiting, and I need a hint or two.

Doorbelllllllllll: They're here! All my girlfriends are here. Let the party begin!

Food and fun, that's what it was all about. We stuffed ourselves with pizza and gulped our soda pops. We found room for popcorn and washed it down with more pop. We got thirsty from all the salt—and slugged back the last of the pop. Yup. We stayed up until 4 a.m. celebrating. Somehow, we never did any levitating and the Ouiji Board left me with more questions than answers. But I'd worry about that tomorrow …. My eyes drifted shut.

I sat up abruptly. "What the ..."

My underpants felt damp. I nearly squealed out loud.
Had IT finally arrived? In time for my thirteenth
birthday? I really was a full-fledged teenager! But,
wait a minute, even my sleeping bag was soggy. I
narrowed my eyes and looked around the quiet
room. Had someone poured water in my bed?

My pajama bottoms were wet. I rolled out of my
dank bedding and dragged it quietly behind me.
Soaked. Soggy. Smelly. Walking like a bowlegged
cowboy into the laundry room, I eased the door
shut, turned on the light, and looked down.

All that soda pop and ... I'd peed my pants!

Peed. My. Pants.

I rummaged in the dirty clothes-basket for
a dry pair of pj's and changed. Trading for a
clean sleeping bag, I stuffed the wet one into
the closet and, face flaming red, slipped back
into the room where my friends still slept.

"Happy birthday to me!" I muttered and
pulled the covers over my head.

RWR

37

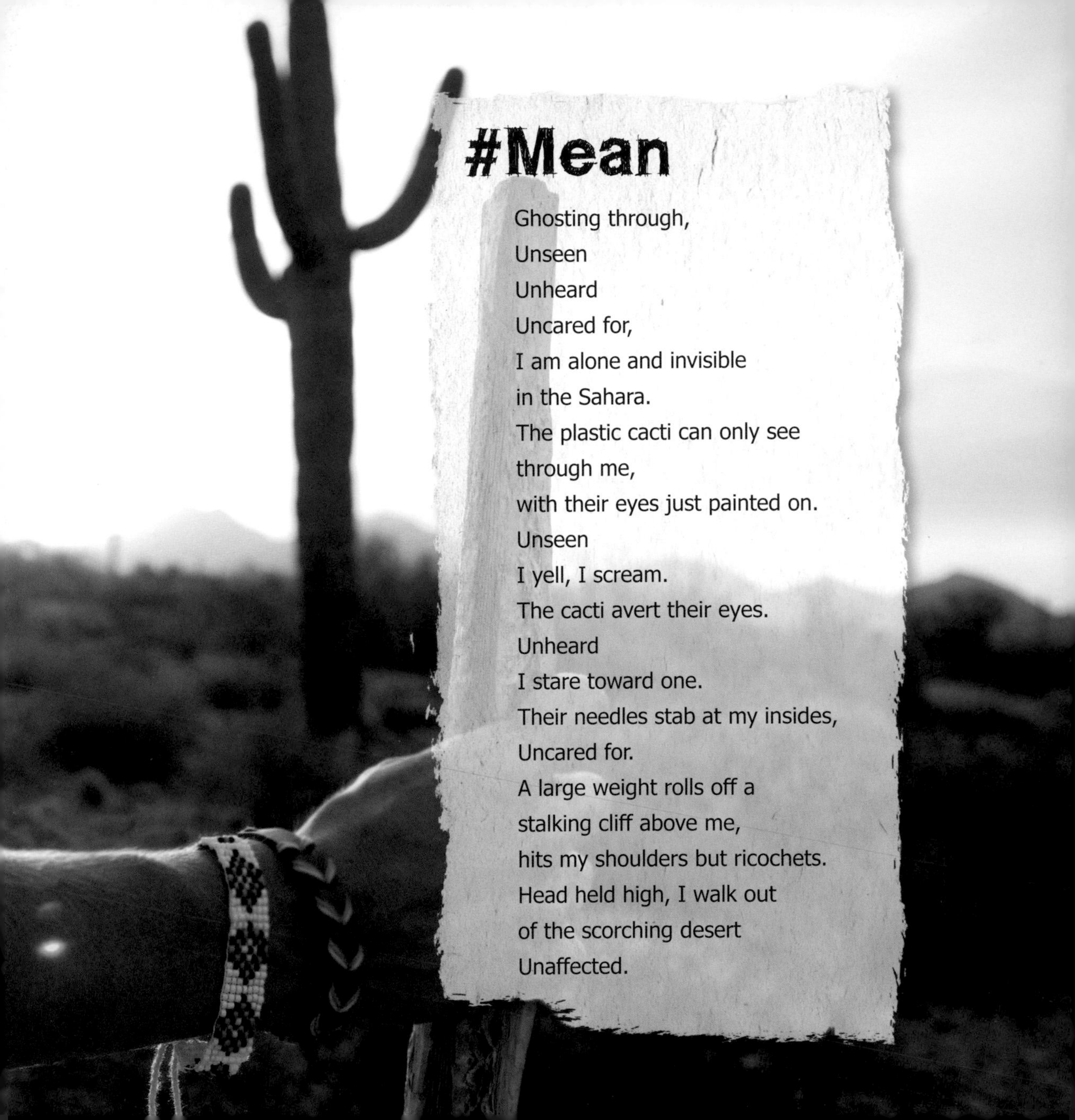

#Mean

Ghosting through,
Unseen
Unheard
Uncared for,
I am alone and invisible
in the Sahara.
The plastic cacti can only see
through me,
with their eyes just painted on.
Unseen
I yell, I scream.
The cacti avert their eyes.
Unheard
I stare toward one.
Their needles stab at my insides,
Uncared for.
A large weight rolls off a
stalking cliff above me,
hits my shoulders but ricochets.
Head held high, I walk out
of the scorching desert
Unaffected.

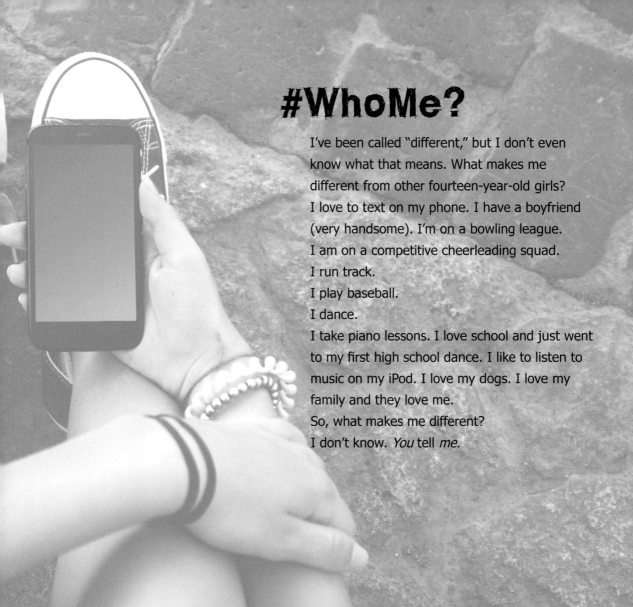

#WhoMe?

I've been called "different," but I don't even know what that means. What makes me different from other fourteen-year-old girls? I love to text on my phone. I have a boyfriend (very handsome). I'm on a bowling league. I am on a competitive cheerleading squad. I run track. I play baseball. I dance. I take piano lessons. I love school and just went to my first high school dance. I like to listen to music on my iPod. I love my dogs. I love my family and they love me. So, what makes me different? I don't know. *You* tell *me*.

#CountryBoy

I need to get me a country boy. The cowboy boot, plaid shirt, camouflage wearin' type of boy.

He can take me mudding, fishing, and hunting. We can take a round in his big green tractor.

On the weekends we'll head down to the lake and have bonfires, listen to country music and watch the stars. We'd lose track of time like we didn't have a curfew.

We will go cruise some back roads in his big bad truck and maybe even get stuck!

Yeah, I want a country boy.

40

#InDisguise

I think it's so fake how some pants have pockets that are sewn shut.
Like, be real with me. Don't pretend to be something you're not.

#Evolution

I embrace my devoted and diligent self. Am I an
overachiever? I really can't tell.
The forgiveness I possess which others exploit and
use to gain access.
The crazy laughter I screech, deafening in a tone
which others cannot breach.
The slow pace I adore, always being careful,
which others abhor.
I embrace the scars on my face which, though
eyes scrutinize, cannot be erased.
The bad luck that follows me; superstitious, is
what I'm perceived to be.
The confusion I express which causes anger and
distress.
The pessimism I portray: "You are so negative,"
people say.
The good or the bad, the happy or the sad, the
pretty or the ugly, I value them all equally.
I embrace my uniqueness, my very presence as I
evolve in self-acceptance.

#Friends

#ZonedOut

"Sing! Louder, sopranos!"

Our volume increased slightly. She wasn't satisfied. She stopped playing and looked at us. With a kind but determined face, our director said, "You need to sing *outside your comfort* zone. Give it all you've got."

Her comment was so profound I could almost hear it convicting us all.

Outside your comfort zone. She was right. I had been singing safely within my comfort zone. I thought about other things I did in life that were within my comfort zone.

I thought about speaking to be heard, just like singing to be heard. What was the point of singing if no one could hear it? It would be just as useless, I concluded, to not speak up for what I believe in. Why have a brain if you don't let people know you use it? Or a heart if nobody can see your passion?

I realized how often I held back just to be safe. This revelation appalled me.

And it wasn't about just giving people an earful. It was about my actions, sometimes the absence of any action. An assertive direction or a firm no. A humble obedience or a caring word.

Things that could mean the world to someone but could also make me just a little uncomfortable. The confidence and sureness I knew I possessed wasn't being used and people weren't getting the whole me. I wasn't giving all I had.

Why would I want to be meek when God had created me to be bold? Why would I want to be generic when I could say, "Hey, I'm Quindelynne!" and then give proof to back it up? I owed it to God—and to me, I reasoned—to be everything that I was. To fulfill my potential and sing louder.

And so I challenged myself to get outside my comfort zone. To go farther. To be more. To step beyond the ideals of the world in order to stand tall as the person God made me to be.

Real isn't how you are made. It's a thing that happens to you. Sometimes it hurts, but when you are Real you don't mind being hurt. It doesn't happen all at once. You become. Once you are Real you can't be ugly, except to people who don't understand. Once you are Real you can't become unreal again. It lasts for always.

-The Velveteen Rabbit

#BrokenGlass

You asked me who I was and, confidently,
I declared, "Myself!" But inside I had
a moment of fear. *Am I mimetic? Am I
pieced together?* I see so many other
people being themselves, so bright, and
I have wanted to be them for so long I
may have become what they show as well.
Yet they, too, would answer with pride,
"Who am I? None but my own self."

We are all patchwork people, elsewise
how would we learn? Silently, they
do as I do, think to themselves about
mosaics made from broken things and
still beautiful. "Myself, the way I knit
myself together." We are all works of art.

#Sisterhood

I love walking through the woods with my sister, catching each leaf as it falls, capturing the beautiful light sneaking between the trees. Long drives are what we do best together, coming off the mountain and heading toward a new adventure. Looking at the beautiful scenery with restless eyes.

There is so much we share, words can't explain. We go from that to this, from this to that, and do whatever comes our way. She knows me too well, but that's what I love about her the most. I am grateful for all of my sisters, each unique. I cherish each step with them.

#GraceNotes

Music is my go-to
when I want to be alone and feel,
when I can be in the moment
to sing, play, write.
Music spills out from my soul and
I can't help but share it.
Music unites us
and fills our void.

#"A"IsFor—

I am proud to be Asian, drowned in all the fame and attention, feeling joy as I receive an "A" for my effort, but shattered as I hear words of discomfort.

"A" stands for Asian.

I feel burdened by my ethnicity as I begin to lose my identity while I slowly acknowledge that grades and race characterize one's self.

You address me by my name, perceive me by my background, but you always fail to understand me and treasure my personality. You fail to comprehend that race explains the ancestor from whom I descended but it never defines who I am: an individual with a distinctive personality.

Now you've crossed the line. You classified me as an Asian with a brain like Einstein and grades of a genius. I despise you for your ignorance and your regard of me as simply an Asian.

I am like no others. And no others are like me. I am uniquely me and not just an Asian.

BROKEN CRAYONS STILL COLOR.

TRENT SHELTON

SOME PEOPLE SEE ME AS A REBEL.

I SEE ME AS A LEADER!

- RENEÉ RONGEN

53

#14YearOldMe

I'm just "one of the guys." I mean, I like my girlfriends—but I luuuv the guys. Ya know? Cuz, with them there's none of the drama and twice the fun! And tonight I'm seeing Jeff. The name I breathe again and again as I do my nightly sit-ups. Jeff. The guy I have a crush on. Yep, Jeff. After I finish my shift at Your Host Drive In, we're meeting at Washington School.

Alone. To talk. Supposedly.

My heart is pounding and I am a wreck. Will I? Will he? Who decides? Is it going to be awkward? Will it involve tongues? Cuz, frankly, that grosses me out.

It's not like I don't have any experience in that department. After all, I did play Kiss-or-Kill in the Bishops' backyard when I was in fifth grade. (I may or may not have always said, "Kill!" when a boy caught me.) Okay, let's face it. I was really not the girl most guys were chasing in the fifth grade. Even then, they needed a ladder just to reach my lips.

Sigh. I sure wish I'd said, "Kiss!" Cuz, had even one of those boys planted one on my lips, maybe tonight wouldn't feel so scary.

Jeff and I met on the playground outside my old elementary school. Idly, we swayed on swings that seemed smaller than I remembered. We talked. We talked about, well, you know. Parents. School. Jobs. We talked about nearly everything without really saying much of anything. Then our conversation drifted to nothing.

We twisted around in our swings, winding the chains tighter and tighter before letting them loose to spin in a fast unwind. As the twirling slowed, I spun back toward Jeff, knowing my swing would bounce off his like a bumper car. Our legs intertwined with every bump. We threw our heads back, laughing up at the stars glittering the sky. At the silly game we played. At ourselves.

The night was perfect.

When our swings twirled back again, Jeff clenched his legs around mine and pulled me closer. His gaze was fiercely intent. He grasped the chains on my swing, lowered his head, and pecked my cheek.

"I like hanging around you," he said. "You make me laugh."

The sultry summer night felt warmer than usual and I was suddenly aware of the heat creeping up my neck and onto my cheeks. That moment was the culmination of my every dream: my first kiss.

RWR

#Remember

Old memories, the ones you
thought were lost in the
darkness, buried in your mind,
stored in the deepest crevasses
of your heart, all come rushing
back at once. You wonder, why
now, when there was nothing,
nothing to set them off? As
you remember the despair and
anguish of your thoughts, before
you remember the memories
you wish you could relive, and as
these thoughts run through your
head you quickly try to re-bottle
them, force them into the darkest
place of your mind, so dark that
as they sink in they become
almost invisible, forgotten forever.

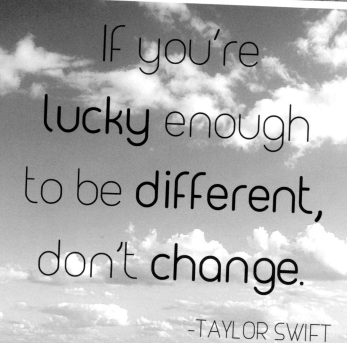

If you're lucky enough to be different, don't change.

-TAYLOR SWIFT

JUST BECAUSE
I AM QUIET,
DOES NOT
MEAN I
AM MAD,
SOMETIMES
I AM JUST NOT
IN THE MOOD
TO TALK.

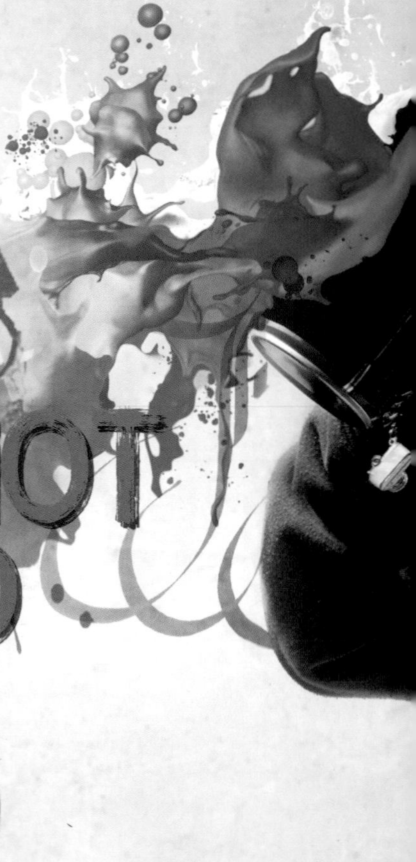

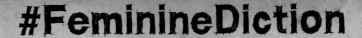

#FeminineDiction

in • gé • nue
[ahn-jha-noo] - noun

an innocent or unsophisticated young woman.

This is my favorite word in the English language. We are all ingénues, whether we are teenage girls or adult women. There is a certain naivety we must all hold onto to remain curious about the world around us, and a certain innocence we must all possess to hold each others' hearts.

#HuggingMyBones

I never felt comfortable with my body.

I was never the little girl everyone easily picked up and carried. I was the little girl who never found a space to hide while playing hide-and-seek, because I stood out. At 5'8", I have always been big. My mother and father are not the skinniest and fittest parents on earth. They're not fat either; they simply have presence. I constantly compared myself to other girls.

When I started playing soccer my sophomore year in high school, I began to lose weight. At first I didn't notice, but my friends would say I was "looking good" and was getting a "coke-bottle figure." Naturally, I liked the compliments. I began to limit what I ate. I don't know how it happened, but I escalated from not eating junk food, to eating once a day, to not eating anything at all. I dropped from 156 to 102 pounds in three months.

The point of my life was not to live, but to survive. My days consisted of avoiding food and forcing myself to perform extremely exhausting and lengthy workouts. My hair began to fall out, my teeth started hurting, and my face resembled a skull. Because I was underweight, my menstrual cycle disappeared.

Every day was torturous. School was a constant obstacle course as I tried not to faint every time I stood to go to a different class; abrupt movement made me dizzy. I shivered to the point of crying because I didn't have enough meat on my body to protect my already fraying bones. My friends tried to feed me, but I turned down whatever they offered. However, I craved everything in sight. I couldn't sleep because my stomach burned, begging for nutrients. I allowed myself a half-cup of water a day. Even though I was hungry, my hands didn't touch a grain of food. I was my own enemy. I had a war in my head, a constant battle against my need to eat. Unfortunately, the side that said no always won.

I felt bitter, troubled, and ashamed because I thought I was fat and disgusting and was never satisfied about anything. In the shower, I cried as I hugged my ribs, traced my hipbones, and felt my spine to comfort myself. I wouldn't go out or enjoy friends and family. Even if I wasn't happy, I was skinny—which made things bearable. I was in profound, deep darkness, and I thought I would never find my way out.

But I did. I woke up one summer day and started eating. I don't know how, why, or what gave me the strength to overcome my mental sickness. The school psychiatrist said it was a miracle, that I am an exceptionally strong person. Not many overcome anorexia nervosa that easily. When I ate, I enjoyed and hated it at the same time.

Now I weigh about 170 pounds. I have learned to be more comfortable in my own skin. Thinking back, I see it wasn't worth it. I wasted seven months, spent slowly killing myself. I missed Halloween, Thanksgiving, Christmas, and Easter that year, moments I will never get back. I spent time fearing the obstacles in my life when I should have been enjoying the things I had. I was the girl who said, "I would never starve myself, people who do that are crazy." But, sometimes, you get caught up in situations and emotions and don't notice what is occurring. I am healthy now. I used to hug my bones, but now what I embrace is my curvier self and the life I am lucky to have.

#AWomanWithin

I will stand up one day.
I will show you that I'm no puppet
and will not do what you say
because I'm a woman within.

I'm here to show you
my power and ability to do
things
you never dreamed of
because I'm a woman within.

I will shoot to the heights
of infinite success and will not
be held back
by your religious handcuffs
because I'm a woman within.

Be it daughter, sister, wife
or mother,
I'll serve my duty
and be strong again
because I'm a woman
within.

Do not forget that I'm the one
who birthed you,
supporting your every step
because I'm a woman within.

Gone are the days when I
bowed my head, hidden
behind the veil
in the four corners of brick
and cement all day, all night
because I'm a woman within.

But remember always, oh dear
men,
no matter how much you let me be
free or hold me back,
I'll always be two steps behind,
to catch and make you stand again
because I'm a woman within.

Clothes aren't going to change the world, the women who wear them will.

— Anne Klein

63

#FindingStrength

One Saturday morning during the final three days of summer vacation, I awoke to screams and yelling. My sisters and I ran to the doorway and watched our parents fighting. Anger throbbed in their veins and narrowed their eyes. They seemed to have forgotten why they loved each other. They focused on why they despised one another. My sisters and I went back to our room. We sat without speaking, a thousand thoughts running through our minds.

Later, I found my mom in her bed crying, hurt, and helpless, unable to utter a word. I knew I had to do something but I was scared, feeling like I was betraying my dad. Finally I called Norma, a close family friend, who told us to quickly drive over to her house. Mom agreed. After we arrived, Mom decided to file a police report.

The officers reassured her that she was doing the right thing, but I was filled with regret. Maybe if I hadn't called Norma this wouldn't have happened. Yet I knew I had to be strong and stand up for my mom and myself. Everyone deserves respect. After a few hours, I relaxed a little bit.

That same day, Mom decided we should move north to Santa Cruz. I was stunned. And nervous. I would have to start over, a new school, new friends, new activities. Classes had already started there, so I would be at least two weeks behind. I'd have to work hard to catch up, but I was willing because it was my junior year and I wasn't about to lose out. We moved in with my grandma in her small trailer. An uncle already lived in one bedroom, my four cousins and aunt in the other. So we slept on the living room floor with my grandma.

Our new lifestyle was a difficult adjustment. It changed my appearance and the way I acted. I stayed inside and didn't feel like going anywhere. I gained a lot of weight, got careless with my dress, and hid my body under oversized clothing. When my uncle said, "Oh don't be jealous of your younger sister just because you're fat," I tried hard not to cry in front of him; I didn't want to show how he'd hurt me. I went outside and bawled. My mom tried to console me but I was angry because I knew it was true.

A few months later, Mom announced that we were moving back to San Diego with my dad. I was excited but nervous about picking up my life in my old school. And I was sad to leave family and the new friends I'd made. Things had changed: Some of my friends weren't there for me anymore, but I learned who was really my friend and who wasn't. I had to determine which classes I needed to get all my credits. It was very tough for me to accept all these changes in just one year.

But I grew. Never letting my personal problems affect my academic life, I maintained a 3.5 GPA. I set a goal and lost twelve pounds to feel better and be healthier. I learned to be strong in any situation, to stand up for myself. Although I'd been sad to leave my dad, I knew there was no excuse for his behavior; violence is never the answer. Unlike the many women who are scared to make a change in their lives, I learned it's not impossible. The struggles and hurdles that beat a girl down can make her stronger and better. I know. I lived it and came out on top.

#WhyTheInnocent?

Lives end prematurely, futures uninhabited, fame never upheld, happiness to come. All halts where men wear masks and their voices bark, piercing the innocent who will not live to see their lives end the way they were supposed to. All their stories suffocated into cold ashes, and buried into graves. Why? Why the innocent?

#TheLifeOfATree

A shower of seeds falls to fertile Earth;
It's life, new birth!
Nestled into its safe, cozy bed,
Excited, yet not quite mature,
The shoot must wait to be fed.
With nutrients and water,
The seedling grows beneath the moon,
Hoping not to become a rotter,
But to grow as large as an elephant soon.
A little more than sprouted,
The slip reveals its first few leaves.
At first we may have doubted,
But the plant is starting to get a lead.
More and more nutrients flow
As the plant begins to steadily grow.

The plant too overgrown
Now becomes a tree
Safely rooted in place.
Humans shout with glee!
The tree stands,
A humble servant
To take blows or commands.
Taking its last breath,
The tree timbers to its final,
continuous rest.
(Also known as an honored death.)
Now carved to the bone,
The tree becomes our sailing ship
And our welcoming home.

#Meanwhile

Why are we always waiting? Waiting for a new episode of our favorite TV show, waiting for the weekend, waiting for a movie to come out ... and once that time has come, we're waiting for the next thing. We miss a lot of things while we're waiting. So stop waiting for tomorrow and live for today!

#Pieta

Though grown, she holds Him close like He's still young
His strength and kindness limp from hatred's scorn
So peaceful—who would know He'd just been hung?
Yet peace comes rough for her to whom He's born.
Her tender cradle rocking even now,
She strokes the marks of nails with gentle tears.
The King was born to wear a bloody crown
And Mary feels each thorn, each whip, each jeer.
She 'til this moment did not understand
The greatest sacrifice: Thy Will Be Done.
She grips so tight, yet with her other hand
Offers to the world her precious Son.
A mother's love is strong enough that she
Would rather it had been her on that tree.

#Perspective

Oh, high school.

Filled with early mornings, crazy teachers, mean girls, hot-and-not guys, mountains of homework, harder classes, gross lunches, annoying people, bullies ... and the list goes on. It feels like you're living a TV drama and, sometimes, you're the star!

So how in the world are you to survive the next four years of your life? Why, you stay strong and push through. Thought I was going to tell you some secret that would change your life and make high school easier, huh? Well, it's actually not a big secret at all.

Some days you don't want to go to school. You're sick; you forgot to study for a test; you're getting picked on. You have to get through your day and brush off whatever is going on. Yeah, I know. Easier said than done.

If you are getting picked on, blow off the crap and melodrama and don't give your bullies a reaction. Otherwise, they get the satisfaction they want and will never leave you alone. What? They say you are stupid-fat-nerdy-ugly-easy-weird-stupid? They insult your race? Phttt. Always remember you are beautiful and amazing in your unique way.

If you're smart, be smart; excel in your studies. If you don't fit in, find others who feel the same. Embrace being you! You don't need the approval of people who don't make you feel good about yourself. Surround yourself with those who support and like you for being you.

When you go to college and carry out your dream career, the girls who picked on you will most likely be living at home, working at McDonald's their whole life. A friend gave me a humorous card when I was going through a rough time at school. The card read: *Dear girls who tormented me in the 7th grade. Because I was smarter than you, I need you to work overtime tomorrow. Sincerely, Your Boss.*

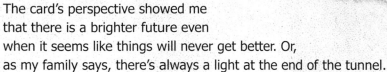

The card's perspective showed me that there is a brighter future even when it seems like things will never get better. Or, as my family says, there's always a light at the end of the tunnel.

"Enjoy high school because they are the best years of your life," people say. Rubbish. Usually, they aren't that great. I strongly believe you should try to enjoy high school—and the payoff happens when you are independent, on your own. The true best years of your life. College, being out in the real world ... it all just gets better and better once you get older. The drama that happens in high school stays in high school. There is a whole world just beyond.

Don't let the pressure and stress get to you. Stay strong. Push through.

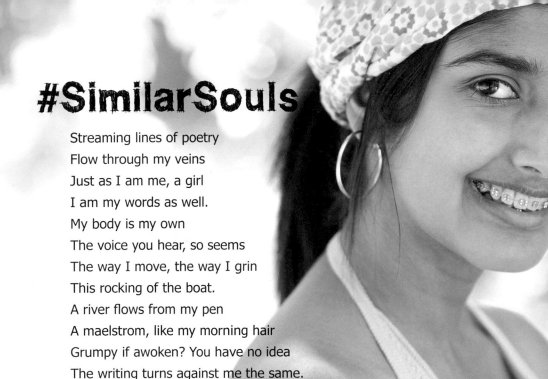

#SimilarSouls

Streaming lines of poetry
Flow through my veins
Just as I am me, a girl
I am my words as well.
My body is my own
The voice you hear, so seems
The way I move, the way I grin
This rocking of the boat.
A river flows from my pen
A maelstrom, like my morning hair
Grumpy if awoken? You have no idea
The writing turns against me the same.
Am I any different from she who
Gesturing, does not write but speaks
Or she who paints her true body, still unsure?
No, I am a writer, yes, I am still a girl.
But of course I am not like them
Friends are those with similar souls
Much like any style, I am who I am
And I, myself, am me.

GO AHEAD, TELL ME THAT I'M NOT GOOD ENOUGH. TELL ME I CAN'T DO IT, BECAUSE I WILL SHOW YOU OVER AND OVER AGAIN THAT I CAN!

#Daddy'sGirl

I know my mom only through other people.

She had huge blue eyes, but horrible eyesight. She had a strong faith and knew God. She was a third grade teacher in a small town and adored all her students, watching in wonder as they learned. She was spunky. She was a huge Nebraska Husker fan. She liked blue and John Deere green. She loved my dad and me more than anything in the world.

We'd been a little family of three: my dad, my mom, and me. Then our world turned upside down when a tragedy changed us to a family of two. I was only twenty-two-months-old when she died in a car accident.

Suddenly, my dad and I were on our own. He was grieving his wife of five years and the mother of his young daughter. I clung to him, grieving in my own way, wondering where Mommy was.

So, Dad and I hung onto each other and made our own way. I was his shadow, his little farm girl, his best helper. I checked cows with him and learned words I wasn't supposed to hear. Or repeat.

We played Uno for hours each night. We lived on eggs, hamburgers, and mac and cheese. He read my favorite bedtime stories again and again as we snuggled with my tattered "B"—the John Deere baby blanket Mom made for me. We ended the day with prayers, hugs, kisses, and lights out.

We cuddled, watching football on weekends. Back then, I loved the cuddles more than the sport. Now, we eagerly cheer our teams together. He taught me how to show a 4-H steer and judge livestock. He taught me life lessons every day. We were inseparable.

As a teenager, I now have a stepmom and two younger brothers. I have grandparents, aunts, uncles, cousins, and friends who surround me and love me unconditionally. And I have my Dad. He is my rock and I am Daddy's little girl!

#LoveMyDaddy

I'm as lucky as can be because the world's best dad belongs to me.

#15YearOldMe

"That's it, Reneé. You're done goofing around
in choir. You're out of here."

Still high from making jokes and getting my friends to laugh again and
again, I wipe the grin off my own face and look up. It's obvious that
Mr. Reichert means business; I'd already been warned plenty of times.

He points to the door. "Study hall. For the rest of the year."

I duck my head to gather my books. I feel
everyone's eyes on me as I walk out.

A cursory glance around the study hall room shows me
I'm with the misfits. *I don't belong with these people,*
I tell myself. Mrs. Lind, the English teacher, is
~~babysitting~~ monitoring us today. She tells
me to journal my feelings. My feelings?

Loser. I scratch on my paper, pressing the
pen harder and harder. *Loser loser loser.*

But I start to find my inner voice as I spew
emotions and thoughts onto page after page,
writing about being the class clown. How it feels
to have others look to you for comic relief, to fill the
awkward silences and the clumsy moments. How being
funny masks my insecurity and pain. *But I know I'm
smart,* I write, *articulate and, frankly, often loud.*

78

On his days to monitor, the speech teacher Mr. Davidson challenges me to funnel my gregarious nature and use it purposefully. He assigns speeches for me to write and give.

"You're a leader, Reneé. Look at how you've won over every kid in this study hall. Now, use that talent wisely. Speak persuasively. Speak out for a good cause."

Mrs. Lind and Mr. Davidson shaped my future. Ignoring my friends' warnings to avoid them at all costs, I eagerly took classes from both teachers (who had reputations for being hard). And I found ways to use what I learned.

Everything really came together for me when I decided to push the novel idea of open lunch at our school. I knew most students and many teachers favored the plan, so I took the initiative to write a proposal. Then I approached the school board on behalf of the entire student body.

"You've taught these amazing kids," I summed up in my presentation. "Now, it's time to trust them! Let them prove you right instead of looking for them to prove you wrong."

I did it. I stood before those adults and persuaded them to consider a cause. Me, clunky-class-clown-turned-serious-orator. Me!

And, the first time we were allowed off campus to walk downtown for lunch? I was high-fived, patted on the back, cheered in the halls. That was the day a *nobody* became a *somebody* by using her talents wisely!

RWR

#InsideOutside

To most this seems like
I'm talking about a room
but for me
it's how I see myself
inside, outside
inside, outside
In my "circle" of friends
this is something they know but with others
that's where the inside part comes

People that I've just met
or those I'm afraid to tell the truth to
I hide inside this
make-believe
closet
But with those who are closer
I'm what you say
outside said
closet

80

Think of all the *Beauty* still left around you and be *Happy.*

~ Anne Frank

#Lemniscate

Sweet child, stay omniscient, stalwart, and cognizant
of the world that surrounds you.
As your adolescence fades away,
keep in mind that fear
is just a word that cannot harm you
and failure is simply trial and error.
Flow through the motions
as Laozi would have wanted,
And if ever you question your morality,
know that comfort is found in the open arms of a loved one.
Never wear your heart on your sleeve,
Never let anyone tell you who you are going to be,
For with every person comes infinite potential.

lemniscate
[lem-nis-keyt]

noun, Analytic Geometry
1. a plane curve generated by the locus of
   the point at which a variable tangent
   to a rectangular hyperbola intersects a
   perpendicular from the center to the tangent.

Equation:
$r^2 = 2a^2 \cos$

Dictionary.com Unabridged.

82

#Fun

83

#PixieDust

I was only five when the nightmare began.

Yellow rotten teeth, holes in his arm, inflamed nostrils.

The yelling, the anger, the punching, the screaming.

The man I knew to comfort me and to

hold me when I had a bad dream,

Was now the man who frightened me.

My father

Was filled with rage and violence.

I was only five when the nightmare began.

I didn't understand what was happening at the time.

I just thought the white powder

he sniffed was pixie dust,

The candy I used to eat with my sister.

I was only five when the nightmare began.

One morning I woke up,

My mom yelling Let's go! and all

my stuff packed in bags.

Hurry, baby, we have to get outta here before he gets home.

I was only five when the nightmare began.

Years had passed,

Scheduled visits.

Three-hour days in the park.

House visits.

To shared custody on the weekends.

More years,

But this time I understood what was happening.

I lost my father once to a powdery substance,

I was about to lose him again.

And to think I was only five when the nightmare began.

Half a dozen months without talking to him,

I still tend to feel lost.

A girl needs her father.

But not a father of his kind.

I am fourteen now.

I'm still living the nightmare.

If the plan doesn't work, change the plan, never the GOAL.

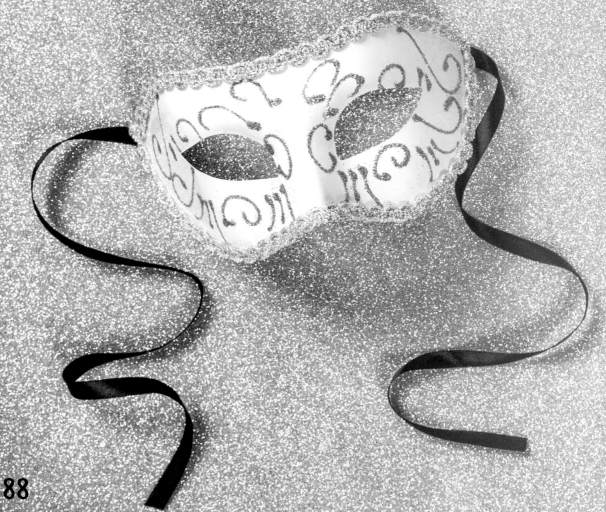

88

#Masquerade

Mirror, mirror, on the wall,
mocking her,
making sure her mask shall never fall.
Only you
allowed to see this girl's true identity,
this game for you a laughing matter,
pure ridicule
a pastime, so much fun.
But she no longer wants to play
for this humor is too crude, too vile.
Just standing there
is not worthwhile
but that no longer is her choice.
Check mate! you call,
your king to hers
with game board pieces all aligned
always aware,
but keep her guessing, keep her blind,
sewing her mask back on,
muffling her voice.

No cries for help are heard tonight.
She missed one tiny intricate detail,
but never expected
nor prepared for her plan to fail
you knew this all along,
that her timing was all wrong,
but your entertainment was not
complete,
not until you knew this was defeat.
So now she stands.
in front of you,
letting all her time fly by so carelessly,
waiting patiently to see when her
mask will be replaced
by none other
than my own face.

#SelfAcceptance

I started when I was thirteen, and I claimed that I stopped countless times. Countless times. I never wanted any of this. Now I'm stuck with it.

I limit myself so people can't see. When I reveal the scars, I ignore the stares, the sad stares that haunt my nights. Some say my actions were dumb; I'd agree. Then again, they taught me a lesson: They restrict me from beginning again.

Some are just finding out; their reactions are worse than my own. Two years of this? How did you manage through two years of this? Rumors ... No, truth. Truth I was too afraid to admit.

I've learned to accept that who I was is not who I am now.

I started when I was thirteen; I ended when I was fifteen. And now I am here for new beginnings.

You have a closet full of clothes,
and never anything to wear.

#BecauseOfHer

Growing up, I always hated the phrase "because you're a girl." It meant I couldn't play baseball on the playground or build small block roads for the toy cars during playtime. It meant I could never be the hero who saved the day. There weren't many girls in the movies, and when they were, they were usually stuck in towers. And I was supposed to love pink and fluff and dresses, just like them.

I looked for a girl whom I could look up to; someone who was brave, independent, and able to find her own way out of a tower. No matter how hard I looked, though, I couldn't find anyone as strong as I wished I could be.

Then my mom got cancer. I was too young to know what that meant, too young to even understand and fear the possibility of death. All I knew was that my parents were scared and things were going to change.

The morning before Mom left to begin chemo, she asked the radio station to play and dedicate a song to us. The lyrics told us that no matter where we were or how far apart, she'd always be with us. We sang along, and I saw her start to cry quietly. I felt cold stains on my cheeks from tears I didn't know I had.

Mom left for Rochester to start treatment, and I waited at the houses of relatives and friends to learn when I could go home. It felt like years between phone calls with her, but I could almost hear her smile on the other end and knew I should try to smile for her, too.

I bolted up, a brilliant idea bursting in my mind. "We can use the bird seed!"

Claire smiled widely, remembering with me the day we found a bin hatch that released a seemingly endless stream of sunflower seeds.

We filled a bucket to the brim with seeds and awkwardly lugged it through our woods to a small clearing. I dug small holes with my hands, and Claire delicately placed a seed in each. When we finished a row, we walked along it, rolling the dirt back into the holes with our feet and covering them in a warm blanket of earth.

By the time we finished our last row, shadows were falling from the trees. We congratulated ourselves and began walking back to my house, our fingers and knees crusted in dirt.

"It shouldn't take more than a week for them to grow," Claire assured me. "I heard my dad say we'd be harvesting sunflowers soon."

"I'd better water them right away tomorrow," I added. We decided to split the profits in half, and Claire promised to think of ways to get the special pickle flavor for our finished seeds.

She left later that night, and I waved until I could no longer see the vehicle, just as I always did. Every morning I carried my watering can to our field and lovingly watered each dirt pile, daydreaming about everything we would do together when we harvested our sunflowers.

School started, but no golden flowers filled the clearing. Snow fell and covered our precious plants for months. I stopped watering them, but still held out hope that someday a sunflower would miraculously spring out of a stale mound. Years passed and we both forgot about our brilliant plans. We didn't stay at each other's houses as often, growing apart in that slow and painful way, like gradually lifting off a Band-Aid. Claire's parents got divorced, and she moved.

There are still no sunflowers in our field. Claire and I haven't spoken in years, and I doubt it would be the same if we did. Sometimes the best plans don't work. Sometimes the sunflowers never grow.

Be a girl with a mind,
a woman with attitude,
and a lady with class.

Be You.

#GirlPower

Fashion is life and makeup is magic. Gucci, Prada, Chanel, and LV to Olay, Dove, L'Oreal, and Dior to Hollister, Versace, Victoria's Secret, and Bon Chic Bon Genre. There is nothing but a deep desire: more.

Gossip is fun and a way to communicate. Clothes, food, movies and songs, schools, home, in and out. Watch out, boy! We're talking 'bout you! Love at first sight, amazing! Holding hands, hugging, and kissing. Sweet three words: I Love You. Forever, together.

Sulking is characteristic, but forgiving is instinct. A sincere apology from the bottom of one's heart is worthier than cash, car, diamond ring. Slim, chubby, tall, or short. Light, dark, or mix. Differences in styles but the same soul. Caring, tolerant, and vulnerable. All need love and to be loved.

We, flowers in a variety of colors and shapes with fragrances to radiate and cover the world, decorating and adorning life. Making it more beautiful. Strong, enduring, and flexible. Surviving in the harshest place, we need only to be caressed and respected.

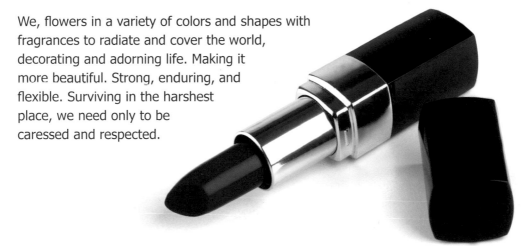

#ChainReaction

One day, during Biology, my teacher stated, "Every action has a ripple effect."

This triggered the light to reality. Imagine all pollinators in the grassland disappearing and, as time goes by, the grass fading and fading, until there is only the impression of a dry and brown surface left. This creates a risk for predators and impacts cause and effect within the whole ecosystem.

The queen bee of a bee colony, she told us, gives a vibe of authority and leadership within her population as the author of life, leading it toward its purpose. That triggering light led me to see that being the oldest of eight is similar to a queen's responsibility: agreeing to maintain a stable and firm attitude, to be a role model for young ones to follow the path I am creating. If I choose to fall and give up, they will learn to do the same, pushing through all kinds of obstacles, like a bee flying through a windy and stormy night.

There will be an end; the night will come to silence and the moon will shine upon the earth. Not until it is over will I rest and continue my task, adopting a new niche in life because my own role models failed theirs and I am willing to resist the urge to follow in their footsteps.

The responsibility demands a determined mindset: Persevere to the end. I will confront obstacles that challenge my weaknesses. Similar to a bee's desire of the sweet and lovely nectar from the prohibited area, there will be temptation, intimidation. There will be those who fall. The production of honey is like the sweet success I strive for.

Leaving the beehive on a beautiful sunny day, sometimes feeling weary or unmotivated, but still producing honey, I will endure to the end. I am the queen of the bee's colony.

#OvercomingSadness

As a sophomore in high school, I was stressed with ACT scores and college applications, classes getting harder, and people getting meaner. Although never bullied, I thought people were judging me. Judging my weird curly hair, lack of fashion sense, weight. Judging everything about me. I suffered with severely low self-esteem. Consequently, going to school each day got harder. Dealing with the same people and the same self-loathing thoughts tormented me.

A deep sadness consumed me.

I tried to be happy. I put on a fake smile and a brave face and never let family and friends see me break. I thought if I hid my sadness from the world it would go away. I fought it alone. It took everything in me to not slip too far down.

All the while, I cried myself to sleep thinking about everything I had done wrong that day no matter how trivial. The next morning I would wake to another day of mistakes. Another night of crying. It was a vicious cycle that even now is painful to talk about.

I was afraid to tell my friends, afraid they, too, would judge me and say I was overly dramatic, life couldn't be that bad. After all, I got good grades, had a good family life, good friends. How could I possibly be sad?

So, I thought I could cry the sadness out. That the moment I ran out of tears, I would finally be happy. I cried until I had no more tears to cry.

But I still wasn't happy.

As the school year went on, everything got harder. Deep sadness became a safety blanket, the easy way out. It was easy to think of ways out of life, easy for me to think, *If I was gone, I wouldn't have to deal with anything. It would be peaceful. I would be happy.*

102

I couldn't let myself do something I would regret (although it did happen a couple of times, I admit). It was excruciatingly difficult to convince myself, *I'm better than this. I can make it through. I deserve to be alive. I deserve to be happy.*

Happiness ... happiness was hard, difficult to reach. I didn't think I deserved to be happy. For some odd reason, I felt I was supposed to be sad and that was that. But I was fed up with it. I looked for anything that could drag me out of this melancholy state of mind.

After searching for something that I could cling to, I finally found it the next summer. I found it in a band. A boy band to be exact: One Direction. And yeah, that might sound super cheesy and lame but it's true. Their music made me smile like I never had before. Their videos and interviews made me laugh harder than ever.

This band became a safety net for me after I had a falling out with a friend or a fight with my parents. When I felt myself slipping into my sad slump, I turned to their music and my moodiness evaporated. They pulled me up and saved me from myself.

Instead of dreading the day, I awoke with a smile on my face. I found an amazing set of new friends that I didn't hide from, that I was able to share my feelings with.

It was liberating.

Sadness is universal. Everyone feels it and it's normal. It's part of growing; some beat it and some don't. My story had a happy ending. I was able to find something that brought me happiness, something that gave me a reason to wake up and to keep fighting. I fought sadness, and continue to fight it, with music. Some fight it with writing, others with reading, dance, art. I've learned not to discredit someone's favorite band or book or actor because that could be the only thing keeping them here on earth.

It doesn't matter how you overcome sadness, it just matters that you do. You don't deserve to be sad. You have a full life ahead of you whether you think you do or not. Stay close to anything that makes you glad you're alive. You're beautiful and amazing and unique. Don't let sadness dim your light. Shine bright.

The
future
belongs
to those
who
believe
in the
beauty
of their
dreams.

Eleanor
Roosevelt

#NightmaresInTheDay

How dare you come upon her and presume to reprimand?
How can you even judge her when you seldom understand?
The thing that bothers me, what I really can't stand,
is how you can just sit there and be so ignorant
to the fact that this girl happens to be an insomniac,
petrified in her bed in them shackles of dread
and fear. But still you posin' here, my little privateer,
sayin' that this girl ain't good enough and sneer.
Yeah, you can call her out in class and say that she's a spaz,
but did you ever think the daydreams are the only dreams she has?

#LiftingMyself

Until three years ago, I was bullied and shunned by people I thought were my friends. The bully became friends with my friends and she turned them against me. I don't know if they were jealous or what it was. To this day some of them avoid me and still won't talk to me. However, I was not going to let them keep me from pursuing my dreams.

As an actress and dancer, I definitely need to stay positive because it can be so easy to feel down when you do not do well on an audition. I started searching for quotes, having my mom get quotes that were framed so I could hang them in my room. I even made up my own for inspiration:

Life is like a roller coaster. Once you're up, you go down. Sometimes there are twists and turns and sometimes there are loops, but in the end you always have fun.

When you judge others, it doesn't prove what kind of person they are; it shows what kind of person you are.

Never try to fit in. If someone can't accept you for who you are, she was never your friend in the first place. So why would you want to be friends with her, anyway?

Some people won't believe in you, some people will. The most important thing is that you believe in yourself.

Take chances and take them again, day after day! Because if you don't take chances, you'll regret and always wonder: What could have been?

If you are having a bad day, just remember: There's a turtle out there somewhere that has flipped on its back and can't get up.

Smile more and worry less. If you spend your whole life worrying, you won't have time to laugh and enjoy yourself.

Are you sad? Are you down? Look for quotes that perk you up. Write them down. Print them off. Post them on the walls of your bedroom. And read them—daily. Better yet, search your heart and tap into your creativity to express your own ideas. Produce original quotes to lift your spirits. And stay positive!

107

#16YearOldMe

I heave and squirm through the tight basement window, shushing the gaggle of giggling girlfriends who are pulling on my arms from the other side. It is 10 p.m. and I'm breaking the rules. Again.

Exhilarated, the four of us sprint down the block and pile into our get-away car like gangsters after a bank heist. Julie slides behind the wheel and points the Pinto toward Main Street while the rest of us laugh and slap each other's legs, giddy with freedom, thrilled with the novelty of new driver's licenses, eager to take a ride on the wild side.

We cruise down Broadway and then back up Main. During one of the loops, I glance at the dingy strip motel that huddled at the curve and get an idea.

"Hey, drive back around and pull into the motel, will ya?"

Like private investigators, we park away from the streetlights to watch who comes and goes. My eyes bug. I gasp and strain for a second look. *Really? Is that who I think it is?*

Yes! We are in agreement.

Aghast, we see her slip into a motel room. With a man. A man who most certainly is not her husband.

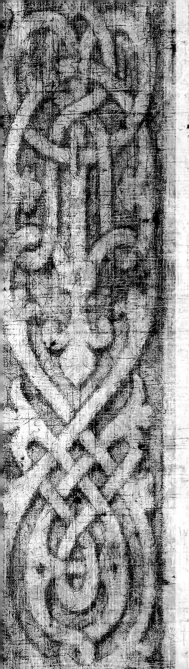

#HowToBreakAHeart

Start like this: smile. And I'll smile back
A swaddled, grinning baby, and you'll sing me a song
And then you go: travel with me in hand, around the world
Marvelling at the flowers, tethered still to home
Next you do this: cook. Dinners upon dinners we have
Enraptured me with variety and all the classics, just you
Simply always: laugh. With a joke on your lips
Or at my antics, after cussing. In greeting and in farewell
It's easy, just: be. Yourself, the force of nature
Friendly and joyous, always whistling, racing about and proud of us
Never forget to: teach. From you I learned all lessons of life
Business, trust, honesty, sportsmanship. Above all else, be kind
And you still: hide your suffering from me
Singing "Please Release Me" as you don't mean home, aged
Going so: fade away. In front of my eyes, and after
I go to the house, echoing of you. Feel you still inside my ribs
This is how you break a heart: strength
In the face of all your trials and I'm trying to do the same
You were so much, and so I'll try. But life is how you break a heart.

#YouAreBeautiful

You can be yourself. You have power in your words. There are others who feel insecure. You don't believe me, I'm sure, but I've been there; I feel you. I've gone through low points, I've been called different, and I bet you have too. Once you truly feel good about yourself, people will accept you. Girls have the strength to pull through anything so don't let people bring you down because of the way you dress, act, or look. You are beautiful the way you are. You are YOU.

Character.
Intelligence.
Strength.
Style.

That's what makes beauty.

— Diane Von Furstenberg

#OnMyToes

I always knew I was different. Just, not exactly in what way. I have Friedreich's Ataxia. FA is a progressive disease that …. It's really boring. Basically, I can't walk, my handwriting is messy, I have a heart condition, I speak with a slur, and I get tired super fast. So, yeah.

I was born November, 6, 2000. My parents were happy and loved me so much. I hit all my milestones on time: eating, walking, talking. I even auditioned to model for Baby Gap because I'm so fabulous! In no time I was starting preschool. I learned to write my name and everything. My teachers noticed I was walking on my tiptoes. My parents thought I was trying to be a ballerina. To be honest, I thought so, too.

When I was four, my brother was born. I wanted to name him Buzz Lightyear but my parents named him Owen. Go figure. Meanwhile, after constant nagging from my teachers, my parents took me for a MRI, a sort of high power X-ray that discovered a tumor on my spine. Doctors said I needed surgery. Worried, my parents agreed. I had just started kindergarten. I was scared, so my mom and dad promised me a puppy after my operation. When the day arrived, I packed my bags and cried all the way to the hospital. Even with the anesthesia, I forced myself to stay awake, so they wheeled me into the operating room that way. But I couldn't fight the anesthesia any more.

I woke in a hospital bed, feeling like fire ants were nibbling on my spine. Somehow, I persuaded the doctors to release me three days later, just in time for Thanksgiving

114

dinner. I went home and stuffed myself with turkey and pumpkin pie, delicious after all that hospital food. And my parents kept their promise: They gave me an adorable pug I named Nelly. After recovering for a few weeks, I went back to school. One day, we went to get my stitches removed. But, upon removing the surgical tape, we discovered I never had stitches—just the tape!

You would think my walking got better, right? Wrong. I got clumsier, my handwriting got messier, and my speech slurred. I got leg braces, X-rays, and CAT scans. No one knew what was wrong with me. During a checkup, the doctor said I had a heart murmur so my mom rushed me to a cardiologist, a heart doctor. He took some blood and ran tests and gave us his diagnosis: Friedreich's Ataxia, a rare progressive disease with no cure.

Only nine years old, I was devastated and confused. After Googling the disease, all I found was a bunch of medical garble like "autosomal" and "recessive," ads for ceiling fans …. Oh, and something called FARA. Friedreich's Ataxia Research Alliance turned out to be an organization that raises money for research. I showed FARA to my mom and asked if we could do a fundraiser. She agreed. So we had a bake sale and raised $500! We continued fundraising, keeping alive our hope for a cure.

In 2012, my little brother was diagnosed with FA, too. I was shocked. How could this happen? I didn't want Owen to go through what I went through, but I watched him acquire the symptoms I knew all too well. Drowning in pity wouldn't find a cure for either one of us, I decided. However, being happy, outgoing … and a fundraiser would. And now I wouldn't be collecting money for just me and Owen, I could fundraise for the 16,000 others around the world who were diagnosed with FA, too.

So that's what I did.

Over the years, I've learned being depressed won't get me ahead in life but happiness will. I don't see myself as disabled even though I use a wheelchair. I'm just uniquely me. We only live once, and I don't intend to waste it.

HERE'S TO THE GIRLS WHO DON'T WAKE UP WITH PERFECT HAIR. WHO DON'T MIND EATING A BIG MAC INSTEAD OF A SALAD. WHO DON'T WEAR 50 POUNDS OF MAKEUP. WHO'D RATHER SPEND THE DAY IN SWEATPANTS THAN SKINNY JEANS. WHO LOVE THE COMFORT OF T-SHIRTS. WHO DON'T GET ALL THE GUYS. WHO AREN'T "POPULAR" BUT FEEL LIKE IT, WHEN THEY'RE WITH THEIR FRIENDS. WHO STICK TO SNEAKERS INSTEAD OF HEELS. WHO AREN'T AFRAID TO BREAK A NAIL. WHO DON'T ALWAYS GET THEIR OWN WAY. WHO DON'T ALWAYS GET EVERYTHING THEY WANT. WHO DON'T NEED A GUY TO TELL THEM THAT THEY ARE BEAUTIFUL. HERE'S TO ALL THE GIRLS WHO ARE JUST LIKE ME.

#BehindTheMask

Why does it matter how I feel?

What you see is real.

As I walk on my path all alone

I take the road less known

Following my life as it flows

Realizing all the friends that are foes.

Trying to fly with the wind

With this distance I would've shined

But now that's just a faint memory

Just like my old love story.

I am never chosen for the lead role;

Deep down that path was never my soul.

Trying to break out of this cage

Finding myself on this stage

Undercover is where I am

Playing a role wherever I am.

I'm a girl with things still unsaid;

I'm plunging forward into the hole that's ahead

While this mask still hides me

From all the pain and troubles that you might see.

#AHelpingHand

One rainy morning, the dark gloomy sky was a warning to stay indoors. Despite the weather, I was determined to get to Rady Children's Hospital. Along with other volunteers, I had committed to help with a Ronald McDonald House charity event by preparing and cooking dinner for families and patients staying there during the winter holidays.

As we arrived, we were assigned jobs. Most girls, including me, hoped to help cook or directly serve the families. However, those positions were limited and there were an ample number of females. Having a passive personality, I allowed others to take on the tasks I desired. Then, the coordinator announced the final openings. "Who would like to be our dishwashers?" She requested two of the forty volunteers, but everyone was silent and hesitant. So, I raised my hand high.

Never able to grasp the fun in dishwashing, I found myself surprised I'd volunteered so readily. Despite my initial hesitancy, I quickly discovered the joy in scrubbing pots and pans when surrounded by families and children happily enjoying the event.

After all the pots and pans were done, we dishwashers were asked to assist other teams. The moment I stepped outside the kitchen, I saw tables filled with children and their families eating meals prepared and served like a restaurant. I headed over to help the baking team, which was positioned beside a sink. I was startled when a family member approached the sink, ready to wash her own dish.

"Wait." I held out my hand for her plate. "Please let me wash it. You're here to enjoy your meal with your family."

She hesitated. Her lips trembled. Her eyes teared. "Why, thank you."

That initial experience at Ronald McDonald House opened my eyes to the world of volunteering. Since then, I've searched online to find and participate in clubs that make a difference in people's lives. And I've learned that it's not the jobs I am assigned that are important but the goals and outcomes of the events themselves. Being able to provide a merry life to others makes my own delightful. Hearing a simple thank you and seeing the bright smiles warms my heart and widens my own satisfied grin.

#BestFriends

My buddy is always there for me
In the good times and the bad.
She always tries to make me laugh,
Especially when I'm sad.
Hysterical, crazy, and a whole lot of fun,
She keeps me right on track.
Like she protects the hockey net,
She always has my back.

Hockey's not the only sport
In which she would excel.
Volleyball and softball, too,
This girl is really swell
I am so blessed to have a friend
Who shows she cares for me,
And my best friend in the Milky Way
Is Kiana Marie.

120

To build a strong team, you must see someone else's strength as a complement to your weakness and not a threat to your position of authority.

Christine Caine

#Drenched

With a bit of annoyance, I close my laptop and grab my shower caddy. I used to look forward to my evening shower; now it is a time-consuming necessity, nothing more. You see, I am currently a college freshman, still trying to adjust to life five hours away from everything I've ever known, and *completely* swamped in homework. Showering is now an annoying part of life that takes away from my studying every night.

I walk down the hall to the bathroom, set my caddy in my favorite stall (number three has the hottest water) and turn on my iPod. The water streams down my back and I'm on autopilot: shampoo, rinse, condition, body wash, shave (ugh), wash face and rinse out conditioner, all to the background noise of my Ron Pope Pandora radio station.

Between my conditioner application and shaving prep, the song changes to "When a Heart Breaks" by Ben Rector, my current favorite. I stop for a moment to listen. Before I even comprehend what is happening, I tear up. I feel so stressed and tired and overwhelmed. I am as happy and excited about my new life as I am terrified and exhausted. My classes are so much harder now, and I don't think I can double major anymore. As these thoughts assault my routine, I lower myself to an awkward, crouched position.

The hot water fails to comfort me. I miss my friends, my parents, my sisters. Especially my sisters. I think of everything I'm missing in their lives and my heart aches. Now I put my head in my hands, as the song continues: *This isn't easy, this isn't clear.* No, it's not easy. I packed up everything I am and started a new life. I left behind so much, and I have no idea what's coming next.

And you don't need Jesus, 'til you're here. It's been two weeks since I've been to church and I feel even worse. I can't ask Him for help if I don't make time for Him, can I? And wow do I need help. I feel like everyone else here has a niche already. Where is mine? I am close to hysteria on the bathroom floor now when I hear: *The confusion and the doubts you had up and walk away.*

And I begin to think of the friends I have made. My neighbor Marissa. She is always up for a girls' night and a life chat. Mikayla, Ruby, Caitlin, Morgan; they seem to genuinely enjoy my company and care about me as much as I care about them. And Josh, the single most amazing person I have ever encountered. All of them love me, and I love them. They will help me get through this.

They walk away …. I wipe my tears and stand up closer to the steamy stream. I smile a bit, hair still full of conditioner. Sure, I'm struggling right now, but this is how it's supposed to be. Everything will turn out okay.

The song comes to a close and I finish my routine, trying to compensate for an unanticipated four-minute-and-fifteen-second distraction. All the release I just experienced shifts to the back of my mind. I focus on the two hours of homework ahead, on tomorrow's exams. Back to the trenches.

Although I won't let myself appreciate it until later, taking a break to freak out, to acknowledge the fact that this new life—although great— is different and hard, was exactly the stress relief I needed. It was a pause, an unplanned pause in time, that allowed me slow down. To stop being robotic. To break routine. To be more than a schedule. I got to be vulnerable, unsure, a human being. Just for a moment.

A GIRL SHOULD BE TWO THINGS:

WHO & WHAT SHE WANTS.

- COCO CHANEL

124

#KickHim

Zap him! Pound him! Beat him down!
Nail the devil, make him drown
In his lies and in his hate.
Make him taste his fiery fate.
Kick him hard and grind him fast,
Give him pain and make it last.
Tie his hands and bind his feet,
Hold his behind to the heat.
He's a thief and a cheating liar;
Throw him in the pit of fire.
That is what he has in store.
Silence him, forevermore.

#17YearOldMe

I. Got. It.

Finally, finally, I got it.

Yes! Yes! Yesssssss!

I lean into the bathroom mirror and inspect my face under the unforgiving light.

Does this change me? Do I look older? More worldly?

I sure feel different, completely changed. After waiting so long, I can't contain my elation. I dance around the bathroom. Slapping my bare feet against the tile. High-fiving the grinning girl in the mirror. Giving whoops that would do any pep fest proud.

I have arrived. I am a **woman!**

I hug myself gleefully (and, if I'm honest, with pure relief).

Frankly, I hadn't been honest for three years.

Since all my friends had "arrived" like, five years earlier, and with my mom urging me to visit a gynecologist … well, I'd felt pressured. So, when I turned fourteen, I lied. I told Mom—and all my friends—that I was finally "surfing the crimson wave." And, through months and months of living-the-lie, no one wasted more female supplies than me.

There had been nothing. Nada. Zilch. Thirteen, fourteen, fifteen, sixteen.

What's wrong with me? I'd wondered. *Am I sick? Put together wrong? How will I ever be able to have children?*

I bottled my secret fears and worries, far too embarrassed and scared to let anyone know the truth.

But, that day, I had finally bloomed—and confidently made my way to the linen closet where Mom kept a stockpile for my younger sister and me.

What? Now, when I really need them .... No way!

"Mommmmmm," I yelled at the top of my lungs, "what happened to all the ..."

What? Me? Go to the store to buy more?

So I did. I marched into the grocery store, selected two large boxes, and carried them like trophies to the checkout line. Nothing shouted "At last!" like those girly-pink boxes, stark against the black conveyor belt. Dancing down the counter, for all the world to see!

Finally. Womanhood. *Honest!*

MY ART IS THE WAY I REESTABLISH THE
BONDS THAT TIE ME TO THE UNIVERSE.
~ ANA MENDIETA

A sweet friendship refreshes the Soul.

~Proverbs 27:9

129

#ColorMePink

Less than one month before my second birthday, my grandma
passed away. She had battled stage four ovarian cancer for four-
and-a-half years, fighting with great courage, tremendous strength,
and steady fearlessness. Soon after, I picked pink as my go-to
color and wore it every day for nine years. Like the pink ribbons
others wear to represent breast cancer warriors, pink was a way
to honor my grandma's life. It showed my personal commitment to
grow up to be as strong and courageous as she was.

Calling someone **FAT** doesn't make **YOU** any *SKINNIER.*

Calling SOMEONE STUPID doesn't make YOU any SMARTER.

All you can **DO** in LIFE is try and SOLVE the PROBLEM in front of **you.**

~ *MEAN GIRLS*

131

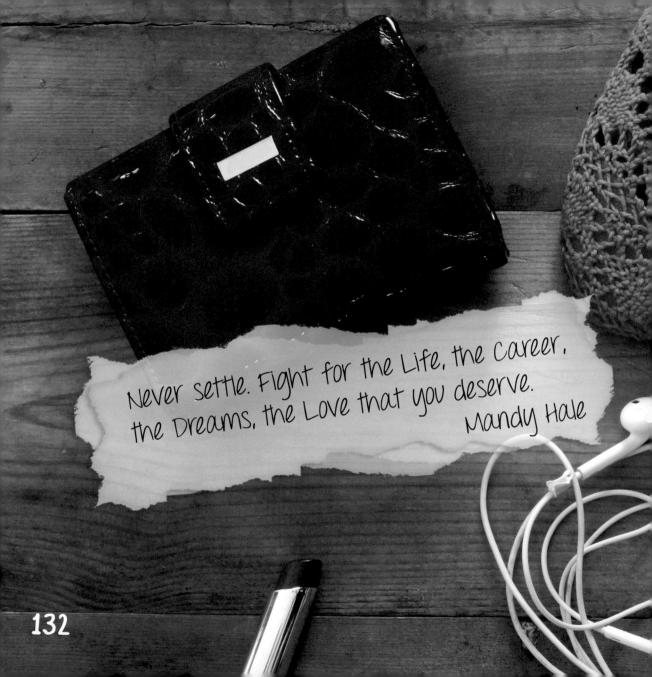

Never settle. Fight for the Life, the Career, the Dreams, the Love that you deserve.

Mandy Hale

#GreatExpectations

Being female sometimes feels like a full-time job. We're expected to get up every single morning, even if we cried ourselves to sleep the night before. We're expected to wear beaming smiles on our makeup-plastered faces, even if we have zero energy and are plain-out crabby.

We're expected to take on the world with determination bubbling inside us at all times. The pressures are always there, like a TV on mute. The busy pictures flash while the sound is inaudible. We're expected to be good, put others before ourselves, have beautiful hair and bodies, work hard, be desirable, and so much more.

Truthfully, it's all exhausting! Why do we worry about all of this? Two reasons: Society encourages us to conform—and because we're girls. That's why.

#FindingMyFunnyBone

I have every reason to give up. To call it quits. Ask anyone who knows me and knows what I've been through. But I don't. Why? I choose differently.

Because I sat at the point of impact in a car accident and suffered a traumatic brain injury, I will most likely have memory problems for the rest of my life. That's sad, but that isn't how I try to see it. If I don't remember something, I make up a story that sounds like it would fit something I would do, had I remembered to do it. I usually make the end of the story so big, so exaggerated, that it is obvious I'm embellishing. For the finale, I admit my forgetfulness. If I was supposed to write a thank-you card and realize that I forgot to do it, I say that I did write them a card and I bought them a new car. I don't really remember, so why not make it a great story? Right?

I could sit around all day just feeling sorry for myself. But I choose not to! I know there are things that I can't do that I could do before the accident. When I dwell on those too much, I feel sad, so I simply don't lurk on the parts of my past that I would change if I could. Instead, I laugh about it, if I can. Humor is always the best alternative.

And, if I can't find humor in the situation, I create it myself.

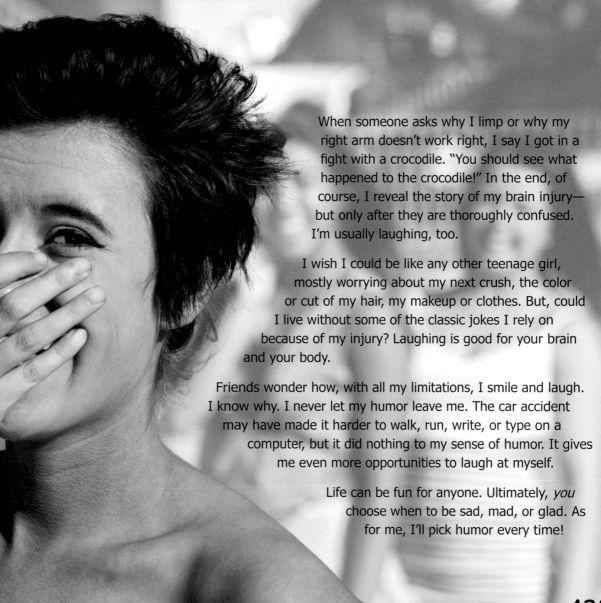

When someone asks why I limp or why my right arm doesn't work right, I say I got in a fight with a crocodile. "You should see what happened to the crocodile!" In the end, of course, I reveal the story of my brain injury—but only after they are thoroughly confused. I'm usually laughing, too.

I wish I could be like any other teenage girl, mostly worrying about my next crush, the color or cut of my hair, my makeup or clothes. But, could I live without some of the classic jokes I rely on because of my injury? Laughing is good for your brain and your body.

Friends wonder how, with all my limitations, I smile and laugh. I know why. I never let my humor leave me. The car accident may have made it harder to walk, run, write, or type on a computer, but it did nothing to my sense of humor. It gives me even more opportunities to laugh at myself.

Life can be fun for anyone. Ultimately, *you* choose when to be sad, mad, or glad. As for me, I'll pick humor every time!

135

#MistakenIdentity

Shot down,
beaten but not broke.
The mistakes I've made
don't define me
but make me.
Don't judge me until
you know who you are.
Learn to live
the life you lead.
Make mistakes
but learn from them.
Embrace being.

137

#Mountain

I'm afraid to go too far one way or the other for fear of getting stuck with no return, to become something I'm certainly not, to be stamped with the wrong sign. I'm afraid to go sour either way. Or to sink.

With no definite path, I'm always gray, a sage who knows to take the middle path, away from the extremes. I'm lost, stuck searching and hopelessly longing for the better side.

I don't (want to) fit in. Seems I don't belong here or there.

Nowhere.

I have no true friends. They're all concerned with matters of themselves and I'm not going to keep on acting like I care. I put on my painted face, clearly mysterious, to keep away from the awkward prospect of sitting alone at lunch, to push further into fake relationships so I don't lose the one thing I'm still searching for.

Maybe it's all connected, all these little choices and these big people?

I don't know, I never knew. But, secretly, I know it all. Always did. I know what goes on between grins across the room. I've seen both sides yet not nearly enough of the other to appreciate this biological evolution called Life. To feel happy without missing a beat of gratitude for the permanently fucked-up world that had no chance.

But I haven't reached that point yet. I don't know if I ever will. It's dark on my side of the mountain.

#MyTerrier

Through the hoops the bounding Boston
goes, over jumps and up A-frames.
Through the tunnels the bouncing Boston
goes, listening to every word I have to say.
Through the chute the bolting Boston goes,
running the course.
Through the weave poles the barreling
Boston goes, only pausing in the box.
Through the maze the bursting Boston goes,
crossing the finish line.
Through the doorway the blithe Boston goes,
sleeping in my arms.

WHOEVER SAID
THAT DIAMONDS
ARE A GIRL'S BEST
FRIEND, NEVER
HAD A DOG.

#BowWow

139

#18YearOldMe

Laughter melts into tears as we hold hands one final time. Using our thumbs, we swipe away smeared mascara under each other's eyes and pinch our cheeks for a little added color. Too soon, we will leave the safety of this close little group.

My girlfriends. Known as The Apostles, the twelve of us have been besties since kindergarten. We know *everything* about one another: the blood covenants we made when we were nine; the number of times we crept out our bedroom windows at night; the secrets we shared as we sat in a circle at the city park; the lies we told to protect ourselves—and each other; the boys we kissed; the rules we broke.

Today we take our final walk down the gymnasium floor. The same floor our sneakers pounded for volleyball and basketball games. Where our saddle shoes jumped in excitement during pep fests and our slippers danced the night away at proms. But this day we teeter in high heels that tap impatiently beneath graduation gowns, setting the tassels swaying on our caps. Most of us wear yellow cords of honor around our necks. And one Apostle, Lori (dubbed LoLo by the rest of us) will be giving the valedictorian's address, profound words I'm certain we'll cling to for the rest of our lives.

After a few more quick hugs, we extend and stack our hands inside our tight little circle. "We can *do* this!" we chant with conviction and turn away to file ourselves alphabetically in the long queue of graduates, losing ourselves in the look-alike crowd.

Pacing our steps to the solemnity of "Pomp and Circumstance," we walked into that gymnasium like we *owned* it. LoLo addressed the class, her memorable speech (which, somehow, I don't actually remember) inspiring her classmates and thrilling her parents. Then, before I knew it, we'd all walked across the stage, received our diplomas and returned to our chairs, a sea of dazed, newly minted graduates.

Days earlier, administration had decreed that we were not to throw our caps in the air in celebration. Really? What harm was there in a bit of hat throwing? I had been waiting for this moment for twelve—count 'em, *twelve*—years. Besides, what could they do? Take our diplomas away?

"Young men and young women," the principal leaned into the microphone, "please change your tassels to the other side of your caps." He smiled triumphantly at his well-behaved grads. "I now present the Class of 1979."

And I made my decision.

The Apostles had always lived on the edge and no one more than me—a polite but respectful rule-breaker. Now was my chance to rebel again.

Under the wide eyes of classmates and fellow Apostles, I grabbed the brim of my graduation cap, hurling it toward the ceiling like a Frisbee, and screamed, "WE. DID. IT!"

Immediately, 175 more mortarboards joined mine. Wowzers!

In that moment, I knew I would no longer be known as an edgy rule-bender; I would be known as a *leader.* RWR

141

Better to see something once, than to hear about it a thousand times.

~ Asian Proverb

#Traveling

new adventures,
opening my eyes to different cultures,
learning people's stories,
experiencing the world,
leaving a part of me in different places,
growing into my own person.

143

#ArtFull

I had no passion for learning. Every day I sat in class, the same tired expression on my face, with only one goal: to complete my homework with my best effort and maintain a high grade. Classmates thought I really loved school, when in reality I was disillusioned. My frustration grew with my disinterest.

But during the second semester of tenth grade, I sat down at the long, brown table in AP Art History. My attention was diverted from the buzz of my classmates to the board where a picture was displayed: A man dressed in a brown cloak stood on the left side, near a window; his wife, in a long green dress, stood on the right side near the bed. *Giovanni Arnolfini and His Bride* by Jan van Eyck.

Why did this painting, out of all I'd seen, appeal to me? I examined the context of the artwork, amazed how the objects and figures—ranging from oranges on the table to a brown dog in front of the couple—symbolized fertility and marriage. The composition told the story of society at the time, depicting the husband as being associated with social life, the wife with household commitments.

Suddenly realizing there was more than just the initial appearance, I began taking an interest in the realism, naturalism, and emotion artists past and present conveyed. And I applied this to other subjects. Where I once saw an assignment, whether in English or Math, as an obstacle to overcome, I now approached it as an adventure with mysteries to uncover and explore. I became engrossed in the journey, more able to express myself without doubt or denial, whether through essays or poems. This re-ignited my interest and passion in learning as I embraced a broader perspective of life and connection.

SELF-CONFIDENCE IS THE BEST OUTFIT. ROCK IT & OWN IT.

146

Find something you're
passionate about
and stay **tremendously**
interested in it.

-Julia Child

#SeeTheWorld

If you close your eyes, if you empty your mind, you can hear the world around you, sharing all that you may find through the wind and through the trees, through the animals of the land or the sea. So open your heart to adventures anew and take that first step forward toward the things you want to do.

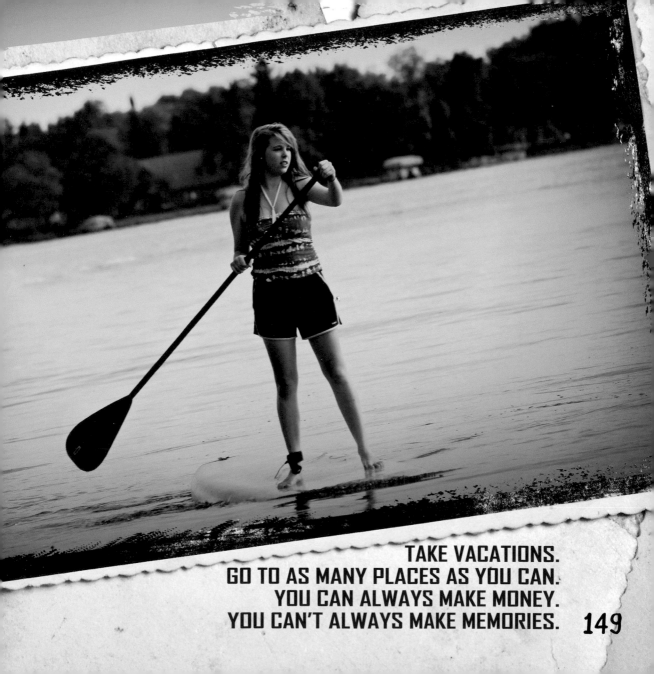

TAKE VACATIONS.
GO TO AS MANY PLACES AS YOU CAN.
YOU CAN ALWAYS MAKE MONEY.
YOU CAN'T ALWAYS MAKE MEMORIES. 149

#It'sAllRelative

My sisters guide me, never give up on me, celebrate with me. They correct me. They challenge me. My sisters are always there to laugh with me. My sisters mold me and expect great things of me. I am so thankful for all three of my demanding sisters!

She is a dreamer, a doer, a thinker. She sees possibility everywhere.

NEVER DATE A GUY WHO DOESN'T HAVE A GOOD RELATIONSHIP WITH HIS MOTHER.

#TakingMeasure

Utterly too big—I wouldn't dare

occupy any space at all, if I didn't need to

yet I'm cringing; rolls slowly unfolding,

I'm spilling into space

I'm not worth wasting

Lugging all of me down hallways

eyes on me; shuffling, waddling

and sitting, arranging

my body around itself, searching

for a comfortable pose, if not a romantically taut one

Reminded everywhere: I'm measuring, comparing,

glimpses in mirrors, tags in the waistbands of last year's jeans

images in my mind, in glossy windows, in classmates' sideways glances

noticing I'm filling up the room

But this boy doesn't know; he's seeing only me

gazing like I'm Ms. Monroe reincarnate

like I am chocolate-covered fruit
softening sweeter inside, cool shell wrapped around
dewy with condensation
Just for now, I can't feel embarrassed to exist
ashamed to command attention
Garnering his looks; I tell him,
those girls whose dainty beauty
I am beastly beside
Of their little bones, he says, "Yeah but
I think if I touch them, they'll just break"
though when he touches me, I'm who's breaking
into thousands of splinters
light enough now to be caught by wind

You are my forever.

~ Kathryn Vigness

A great attitude becomes a
GREAT DAY which becomes
a GREAT MONTH which
becomes a GREAT YEAR
which becomes a GREAT LIFE.

Mandy Hale

#OtherHalf

Hair braided back, lit by the moon,
She finds herself dancing outside of her room.
She twirls and she twists, her feet skim the ground,
All without ever making a sound.
She flits to the window—she comes here each night,
Disguised as a shadow or fragment of light,
To sing to the child on the other side
Whose doctors had failed although they had tried.
That girl-child sheds many tears at night,
Trapped in her body in endless flight.
Who would've thought that just one little chair,
Could cause a damage no one could repair?
That is the reason the dancer is there.
The girl on the outside dances tonight,
Each leap and each turn, putting forth all
her might,
Hoping against hope to make wrong into right
Inside that broken soul.
For she and the child were one and the same,
Before tragedy struck, leaving no one to blame.
They both lost what they could not regain;
The damage that broke them in two remains.
The girl tries to make her other half smile,
Knowing she must go away for a while;
Only when she's needed most
Is she permitted to ever get close.
So as the sun gives the new day its best,
The young ballerina is left to rest.

#Contributors

#Artists

* CONTRIBUTORS' AGES REFLECT THE
  AGE AT THE TIME OF SUBMISSION.

Reneé Rongen

www.reneerongen.com
Renee@reneerongen.com

#MeetReneé

Renee Rongen, known as the mother of motivation for her signature Legacy Living Philosophy, inspires others to live life from the inside out. She is an award-winning entrepreneur, international speaker, author of the coffee table classic *Grandy's Quilt…A Gift For All Seasons* and *Fundamentally Female*™ Dubbed by media as a "vibrant blend of Oprah, Lily Tomlin, and Mother Teresa," Renee is a master of comedic timing, taking her audiences on an emotional roller coaster they never forget. With a heart for giving back, Renee has established the Ultimate Pajama Party™ which has donated close to one million pajamas to domestic violence shelters across the world. This wise, witty, and sometimes feisty mom of adult children Alex, Elizabeth and Grace, lives in Northern Minnesota with her husband Tom.

Renee loves to hear from hear from her readers. To learn more about her speaking availability, book signings, Ultimate Pajama Party™ and discover the authors and artists featured in this book, visit www.reneerongen.com.

"So much more than a Speaker or Author… Reneé is an Experience!"